THE KING ENTREPRENEUR'S GUIDE

DOING BUSINESS GOD'S WAY

SHAE BYNES

AUTHOR OF *GRACE OVER GRIND*

The Kingdom Driven Entrepreneur's Guide:
Doing Business God's Way

Published by Kingdom Driven Publishing
4846 N. University Drive #406 | Lauderhill, FL, 33351 USA

KingdomDrivenEntrepreneur.com

Interior Design | Cover Design
DHBonner Virtual Solutions LLC
www.dhbonner.net

Published in the United States of America

ISBN: 978-0-9996763-2-5

DEDICATION

This book is dedicated to my sister in Christ, my dear friend, and Co-Founder of the Kingdom Driven Entrepreneur movement, Antonina Geer.

Antonina, without you, this book would not have been written.

Had it not been for your willingness to share those three words in your journal "Kingdom Driven Entrepreneur" with me in June of 2012, we never would have embarked on a journey together to see a dream that was on God's heart come to life. I personally would have missed out on what has already been the adventure of a lifetime.

I will forever honor you for your obedience, your heart for the Kingdom, and your selflessness. Thank you for being you. I love you so much!

Contents

ACKNOWLEDGMENTS

Thank you, Phil Bynes, for believing in me and supporting me in pursuing all that God has destined for me. We make a great team, and I give our Daddy (Abba) all the glory for it!

A huge thank you to my partner in publishing matters, Desireé Harris-Bonner, for your brilliant work that is consistently done with excellence.

Thank you, Jesus, and thank you, Holy Spirit, for inspiring my teaching, guiding my writing, and preparing receptive hearts to receive Your message, which is the power and the goodness of an adventure in business with You and Your glorious Kingdom at the center of it all.

INTRODUCTION

In November 2012, Antonina Geer and I, two complete strangers divinely brought together by God, launched a movement called Kingdom Driven Entrepreneur. It started with a simple word from the Lord five months prior: "It's a community, it's a movement, and it starts with a book." There we were, two entrepreneurs with a heart to please God and to be obedient to an assignment that neither of us on paper was qualified for. Qualification in the Kingdom surely looks different than it does in the world!

Armed with that one revelation and instruction, we put our faith into a corresponding action and started to work on a book which was eventually titled and released as *The Kingdom Driven Entrepreneur: Doing Business God's Way.* With the release of the book came the beginning of a global online community and it truly has been one wild, crazy, and amazing adventure ever since. God transitioned Antonina out of the operations of the business in 2015, and I've had the honor of continuing this Kingdom marketplace assignment and expanding the organization (online and offline) in full partnership with Him.

We've since grown to be a powerful team of ten - thank you, Jesus, and thank you, Team KDE!

Several thousand entrepreneurs around the world have

read and been inspired by the message found in the pages of that first book, but two years ago, a desire rose up in my heart to release a fully revised version. I felt like God confirmed that it was indeed a "God idea," but one that was ahead of His timing.

Instead, He led me to complete another book, *Grace Over Grind: How Grace Will Take Your Business Where Grinding Can't*. No sooner than a few months after releasing Grace Over Grind, I received the green light to write this book, *Doing Business God's Way* for Kingdom Driven Entrepreneurs.

So here it is, another labor of love. There's little from the original book in this fully revised edition, but the heart and spirit from which it has been written is the same. My prayer is that as you read this book, you will feel inspired and equipped to both grow and thrive as a Kingdom Driven Entrepreneur.

1

THE HEART OF A KINGDOM DRIVEN ENTREPRENEUR

*"But seek first the kingdom of God
and his righteousness, and all these things
will be added to you."*
—Matthew 6:33

This is a Kingdom Driven Entrepreneur's guide to doing business God's way, so we need to start with defining what a Kingdom Driven Entrepreneur is and how it may be different from what you're accustomed to experiencing among believers in the business world.

Kingdom: God's rule and reign (the King's way of being and doing things), the realm of Heaven, and the government of God

Driven: Propelled or motivated by

Entrepreneur: One who organizes and operates a business (or businesses), identifying a need or desire and filling it in the marketplace

When we talk about being a Kingdom Driven Entrepreneur, it means that your entrepreneurial endeavors are motivated by seeing an increase of the Kingdom of God on earth, and they are propelled forward by seeking first the Kingdom of God and His righteousness.

When you are a Kingdom Driven Entrepreneur, it is certainly not business as usual. Your business is fully yielded to God (the Ultimate Chief Executive Officer) and guided by Holy Spirit (the Ultimate Chief Operating Officer). You allow Jesus Christ to be Lord of your entrepreneurial journey by putting the King's agenda first. You transition from a heart of, "Here are my plans, God. Bless them!" to a heart that is aligned with God's dream for your business. You seek His heart for the people you serve and cross paths with in the marketplace.

When you are a Kingdom Driven Entrepreneur, you are no longer satisfied with profiting in business by doing it the world's way and then using those profits for funding the gospel. You will not be content with hanging scripture verses on the walls of your office or establishment, putting a "Christian owned" decal on your door or website, or naming your business based on a biblical theme or concept. While there is nothing inherently wrong with those things, they will feel inadequate for you.

The truth is that you can be a believer and follower of Jesus Christ, operate your business based on sound biblical wisdom and success principles, and yet still not be primarily driven (motivated and propelled forward) by the Kingdom of God. You can build a financially prosperous business based on those principles without experiencing an authentic relationship with the God of those principles.

Being a Kingdom Driven Entrepreneur is simply not the same thing as being a Christian who owns a business. As an entrepreneur, you can be driven or led by a variety of things. Some are driven by profits, accolades, power, passion, or freedom and flexibility, but the Bible shows us that to experience God's best, we should be driven by the Kingdom of God and led by the Spirit of God. In fact, it gives you an advantage!

My friend, Dr. Jim Harris, author of *Our Unfair Advantage,* shares, "It's a monumental leadership transformation to go from being Head-led, Money-led, Innovation-led, Opportunity-led, Price-led, Pressure-led, Feelings-led, and Pride-led to being fully and only Spirit-led. [We] have a co-witness living inside us, the presence of God upon whom we can call upon, seek out, ask, inquire of, and be led by anytime...anywhere.

It is a distinct competitive advantage because it is based upon one and only one thing: from you being led by the What

3

(the things of the world) to the Who (the Spirit of God)!'"

Once you decide to be a Kingdom Driven Entrepreneur, you simply will not be able to imagine doing business without partnering with the presence of an awesome and limitless God. Isn't it an honor to know that the Creator of the Universe, the only one who sees all and knows all is interested in working with you in your business? He desires to create with you, guide you, provide for you, and draw you (and others) closer to Him in the process.

A Different Kind of ROI

You are likely familiar with the concept of Return on Investment, or ROI. According to Investopedia.com, ROI is a performance measure used to evaluate the efficiency of an investment or compare the efficiency of a number of different investments. ROI tries to directly measure the amount of return on a particular investment, relative to the investment's cost. It is a key financial measure for a Kingdom Driven Entrepreneur (unless God tells you it's not), but even more important is the eternal ROI of your business.

As a Kingdom Driven Entrepreneur, your ministry is business, and your business is ministry. You are a minister in the marketplace in service unto God and unto others. God has a vision for your business that He is faithful to reveal because He has His creation—the entire universe and everything within it, including us—on His mind. Know that there is an eternal impact in your business and your strategic day-to-day business decisions. It is not solely about your business finances or even the standard of excellence that you are committed to, but it is about the glory of God revealed on the earth through the work that you do.

The eternal impact is transformational impact on individuals, families, industries, and communities. It is bringing light to areas of darkness. Jesus said, "I came that they may have life, and they may have it more abundantly." (John 10:10). Life is *zōē* and represents a life that is authentic, active, vibrant, devoted to God; the absolute fullness of life that is an expression of Him on earth.

As a Kingdom Driven Entrepreneur, you have the opportunity to get involved with what the King is doing. The Kingdom of God is at hand, and the more you experience it personally, the more you will be able to influence the world around you. You have the privilege to be actively involved in seeing His Kingdom ever increase and seeing the fruit of many coming into personal relationship with Christ as they encounter His glory.

The Countercultural Ways Of The Kingdom

> *"And Jesus came and said to them, 'All authority in heaven and on earth has been given to me.'"* –Matthew 28:18

In order to thrive as a Kingdom Driven Entrepreneur, you must acknowledge and embrace that the Kingdom of God looks nothing like the kingdom of the world (or kingdom of darkness). These are two different spiritual kingdoms; you and I must align our minds and posture our hearts toward the realm that is created and governed by the King of kings, Jesus Christ. The Kingdom of God is a government all by itself. It is not a republic or a democracy that is ruled by the people.

The King is in charge, His way rules, and your primary citizenship resides in His Kingdom, not the country in which you physically reside.

The beauty of this model is that the King, in His absolute authority and sovereignty, is perfect! He rules with love, grace, and justice. You can trust His rule completely. You can operate your business without fear in a manner that is subject to His rule and His way, even when it flies in the face of everything you encounter around you or does not make sense to your rational mind.

Here's a sampling of the instructions we get for Kingdom living directly from the King that run counter (in some ways quite radically) to the ways of the world:

- Deny yourself. Take up your cross and follow Jesus. (Luke 9:23-25)
- You cannot serve both God and money. Serve God. (Matthew 6:24)
- Don't be anxious about your life, worrying about the

basic essentials of living. (Matthew 6:25-32)

- Pray for and speak words of blessing over those who persecute you. After all, if you only love those who love you, what is the difference between you and those who are not sons and daughters of God? (Matthew 5:43-47)
- Speaking of persecution, rejoice and be glad when it happens! (Matthew 5:10-12)
- Give to the one who begs from you, and don't refuse the one who would borrow from you. (Matthew 5:42)
- Turn the other cheek. If anyone sues you and takes your tunic, let him have your cloak as well. Someone forces you to go one mile, go with him for two. (Matthew 5:38-41)
- There's a wide path to destruction. Don't follow the masses. Choose the narrow gate. (Matthew 7:13-14)
- Serve the poor and show compassion to the "least of these." (Matthew 25:41-46, 9:9-13)
- Become like a child so that you may experience the Kingdom. (Matthew 9:13-15)
- Don't condemn people. Jesus isn't in that. (John 8:11)

I suspect some of these made you uncomfortable, and perhaps even made you want to debate what Jesus really meant when He said what He said. I get it. Quite frankly, a couple of these make me uncomfortable too, and God is still working on me! However, when we honor the ways of the King and put His agenda first over our own as we run our businesses, we position ourselves to experience God's best. We release the power of the Kingdom into the lives of others and provide them with an encounter with the One who conquered sin and death to restore humanity into right relationship with the Father.

When you seek first the Kingdom of God and His righteousness in your business, everything that you need will be added to you. This does not mean that it is always what you think you need, or that it comes in the time you think you need it, or that it arrives via the avenue you think it should come. Part of the adventure as a Kingdom Driven Entrepreneur is learning how to lean into the character of God and place your trust in Him.

Throughout it all, you can enjoy righteousness, peace, and joy that the Kingdom provides. The Kingdom of God has many benefits and privileges, and it's God's pleasure to give them to you.

> *"Fear not, little flock, for it is your Father's good pleasure to give you the kingdom."*
> —Luke 12:32

We've established that doing business God's way is counter-cultural to the world's way of doing business. You may find that there is a mountain of things for you to unlearn about how to operate as an entrepreneur.

Don't be overwhelmed by this—it's normal. It seems that every year I identify yet another mindset I must unlearn that I carried over from investing in education on how to start and grow a business from worldly experts (and even Christian experts who are operating in worldly principles) for over a decade.

In the pages that follow, you'll discover more about how to grow as a Kingdom Driven Entrepreneur. We will begin with what I believe are the two key foundations that lay the groundwork for developing a lifestyle of being led by God in the work that you do in the marketplace: *Intimacy with God* and *Radical Faith and Obedience.*

REFLECTION QUESTIONS

1. How would you define the Eternal ROI of your business?

2. When was a time that you handled a situation in business in a way that was not in line with Kingdom principles? How could you have handled it differently with God's help?

2

INTIMACY IS EVERYTHING

The God of the Universe desires to have a personal and intimate relationship with you. Pause and let that statement rest in your heart for a moment. This is one of the most awesome invitations we have from God, Abba Father—to enjoy a nearness with Him through Jesus Christ, through His Word, and through His Spirit dwelling on the inside of us.

> *"Draw near to God*
> *and he will draw near to you."*
> —James 4:8

The Kingdom of God is a government, but how can you seek first the Kingdom of God and His righteousness without knowing the ruling King? You can't even know yourself without intimacy with the King. It's through the abiding fellowship with God in Christ that you are transformed from the inside out. It's through intimacy that your mask falls off, layer upon layer; you get to know who you truly are and then the world is blessed with getting to encounter the unique expression of God that is you.

I was raised in a loving Christian home with parents that were very active in the local church. When I left home at age 18, I read my Bible on occasion and found a church to attend regularly throughout the duration of my college years. I then got married and committed my union to the Lord. I was sensitive to the voice of Holy Spirit. I knew God's voice (although I was not always receptive to hearing Him), even as I was living an achievement-driven and performance-based life.

It wasn't until age 35 that I yearned for experiencing more of God in my life. I didn't want to know more *about* Him; I wanted to *know* Him and to *know myself in Him.*

I'll never forget the radical encounter with God that ignited an authentic intimacy with my Father, with Jesus Christ, and with Holy Spirit. I traveled to Orlando to attend a women's conference, and on the last evening of the conference, Pastor Cynthia Brazelton ministered on intimacy with God. She asked us to close our eyes while she asked God to help us to know Him in a more intimate way. She asked God to give us spiritual eyes to see and spiritual ears to hear.

Then she was quiet.

A couple of minutes later she asked us to stand up if we heard anything. I hadn't heard anything but silence. Then she asked us to stand if we saw anything. I hadn't seen anything either. There were all these women in the room who were standing. My heart cried out to God with a bit of angst, "Show ME something, Lord!" In that moment, there was nothing I wanted more than to experience more of His presence in my life.

Nothing happened. Pastor Cynthia moved on and shared her closing remarks. I honestly cannot remember what she was talking about, but what I do remember is unexpectedly falling to the floor. I face planted right on my friend's white high-heeled shoe. I didn't understand why I was on the floor. I tried to get up, but I couldn't move. It was as if my entire body was glued to the floor with rubber cement and an angel was sitting on my back. I felt awkward and horribly self-conscious. I wondered what the people who were around me were thinking. "Why am I on this floor? Lord, let me up!"

Nothing. I still couldn't move. I struggled for what seemed to be an eternity and then decided to stop because it was clear that I wasn't going anywhere. I said to God, "Ok, you have my attention. What do you want to tell me?"

At that moment, I experienced an open vision for the first time in my life. It was like watching a movie. God showed me a vision of me playing the Trust Fall game as a child. The purpose of the game is to trust that the person standing behind you will catch you when you fall. You close your eyes and fall backwards and hope for the best.

In the vision, God showed me falling backwards, but at the last moment taking control by putting my hand back to brace myself in case of a fall. I heard His voice say, "That's what you do to me." I felt stunned and convicted, but not at all condemned.

He whispered to me: "Do you know why you do that?" I responded, "No Lord, why?" His response: "Because you have absolutely no idea how much I love you." The rubber cement disappeared, and I was able to get off of the floor. I thanked God for showing up and sharing with me in such a clear way, and I went back to my hotel room to go to bed.

The next morning, I woke up early. My conference roommate (the one whose shoe I had landed on) was awake, so I shared more about what had happened the evening before. I was in awe over the entire experience, and we sat there in our beds talking about the goodness of God.

In the middle of our conversation, a heaviness fell in the room unlike I had ever experienced in my life. There was a tangible, weighty presence of God's glory in that hotel room and all either of us could do was weep and get on our faces and worship Him. As I worshipped Him, He showed me another vision.

He showed me a hand. The hand was opening and closing repeatedly. The Lord said to me, "This is what man does. Sometimes His hand is open to you; sometimes it is closed. This is what you think that I do, but I am not man." He then showed me two open hands and said, "THIS is me. I love you, and my hand is always open to you. Everything you need I have and am willing to give to you."

Over the next two weeks after the conference, I experienced signs, wonders, and miracles in my life that I had never experienced before. With each encounter, I felt God whisper to my heart, "See how much I love you!" This experience changed my life forever; I pray that I never grow tired of telling that story and that it always keeps me in awe of our amazing Father.

Intimacy is everything and is the foundation of your operations as a Kingdom Driven Entrepreneur. What I discovered about intimacy with God is that it strengthens trust in Him and His promises. Intimacy creates trust, and then trust creates even greater intimacy.

It's a beautiful progressive cycle that takes us from one level of glory to the next level of glory.

The Power of Intimacy in Business

"I am the vine; you are the branches.
Whoever abides in me and I in him,
he it is that bears much fruit, for apart
from me you can do nothing."
—John 15:5

"So Jesus said to them, 'Truly, truly, I say to you, the Son can do nothing of his own accord, but only what he sees the Father doing. For whatever the Father does, that the Son does likewise.'" –John 5:19

Jesus Christ demonstrated through His life on earth the power and necessity of maintaining an intimate relationship with the Father. Additionally, Jesus revealed to His disciples the power and necessity of abiding in Him, the true vine.

You want your work in the marketplace to bear much fruit? The solution is to abide or keep company with Jesus. Want to experience the fullness of what God has on His heart concerning your life and business? The solution is to see what the Father sees and then go and do that.

Here are some of the benefits of cultivating a personal and intimate relationship with your Ultimate CEO and the best business partner you will ever have:

Firmly rooted identity in Christ. The more you commune with the One who created you, the more you see who you truly are. Intimacy reveals identity. Identity brings freedom.

Ability to discern God's voice. Jesus said, "My sheep hear my voice, and I know them, and they follow me." Heaven is always speaking and intimacy positions you to hear what the Spirit of God is speaking to your heart.

Alignment of your desires with God's. The Bible tells us in Psalm 37:4 that when you delight yourself in the Lord,

He will give you the desires of your heart. Through your intimacy with the Lord, He places (puts upon you) the very secret petitions and prayers on your heart. Your dreams and desires align with His will and His thoughts concerning you. There is no better place to be.

Rest instead of striving. Fellowship with Jesus and enjoying the presence of God allows you to stay in His rest, to work in the unforced rhythms of His grace without burden, anxiety, overwhelm. Fellowship helps you stay in lockstep with Him.

As an entrepreneur, your desire is to get things done, and sometimes you can get ahead of God. When you have intimacy, you will receive course corrections that will get you back on the right track (without shame or guilt) and help you progress in business at the pace of His grace. God also empowers you to get wealth (Deuteronomy 8:18) and grow in profitability in your business in His rest without sorrow and without anxious toiling!

Ability to maintain pure motives. Selfish ambition is a sneaky little beast; one that is easy to fall prey to, even for a sincere-hearted Kingdom Driven Entrepreneur. After all, the world of business looks favorably upon ambition and the drive to be the best and achieve more. Shouldn't you want more for your business? Won't greater influence, profits, and prominence mean a greater impact for the Kingdom of God?

17

According to the scriptures, not necessarily. Ambition that is not honoring and surrendered to God (selfish ambition) can easily lead down a path of destruction. Intimacy purifies our hearts and purifies our motives.

Peace that surpasses all understanding. There is no peace that is like the peace of God. When there is every natural and logical reason to be frustrated, upset, or worried as you face various challenges and trials in your business, the peace of God allows your heart not to be troubled. You experience a quietness in your spirit that simply does not make sense.

I am fully convinced that we cannot experience true peace until we've not only encountered the Prince of Peace, but we also are willing to pour out our hearts to Him authentically and renew our minds through His word.

Access to God's secrets. Intimacy develops friendship with God, and it is in that friendship that you receive greater revelation and secret counsel. Psalm 25:14 (NKJV) says "The secret of the Lord is with those who fear Him, and He will show them His covenant."

Dr. Brian Simmons expressed the goodness of this friendship beautifully: "There's a private place reserved for the lovers of God, where they sit near him and receive the revelation-secrets of his promises. Those are the ones He tells His secrets to" (Psalm 25:14, TPT). Every Kingdom Driven Entrepreneur should crave this level of friendship with God where His secrets are revealed.

Cultivating Intimacy with God

"For he satisfies the longing soul, and the hungry soul he fills with good things."
—Psalm 107:9

Cultivating intimacy (closeness) begins with a desire; a hunger and thirst for more of God in your life. I've found in my life that there is no hunger that Jesus Christ fails to satisfy.

When I was sitting in that women's conference in Orlando in September 2012, my soul was longing for more. At that time, I had already left my comfortable, high-salary-paying corporate career two years prior out of obedience to His instruction. I had already said yes to the assignment He had given me to begin Kingdom Driven LLC and launch the Kingdom Driven Entrepreneur community and movement with Antonina Geer, a woman He had just introduced into my life.

Here I was making the hard decisions to say yes to things that made no sense because I could not deny what God was speaking to my spirit, but I also knew that my highly-analytical, meticulous planning, achievement-oriented self was not going to be able to do anything without knowing

Him in a deeper way. When my soul cried out, He responded in the most beautiful way that night in Orlando and during those weeks after the conference.

When you are primarily achievement-driven like I was at that time in my life, it is easy to believe that getting close to God requires creating a checklist of "Good Christian things to do," but what I found is that it is not at all about a checklist. It is about intentionality and vulnerability. When I reflected on what the journey to cultivating intimacy looked like in my own life, three elements emerged:

1. Getting to know Him,
2. Unveiling myself to Him, *and*
3. Practicing an active awareness of His presence.

Getting to know Him

It was important to get to know God's heart, His character, and how He operates by investing time reading, studying and meditating on the scriptures. This is not a mere intellectual exercise, but it is an encounter with the living God. It is not just about obtaining wisdom and getting revelation of principles, but allowing this divine love story to reveal the three Persons who are each fully God—Father God (Abba), Jesus Christ, and Holy Spirit—to you in a deeply intimate way.

While reading the scriptures, have a conversation with

God. Ask questions and ask Holy Spirit to give you a greater understanding on how it applies to you, your life, or even your business. I have often asked "What do you want me to take from this?" and I like to read multiple translations and use references to see what the words and definitions in Greek or Hebrew are because in the process of doing so, He reveals new layers and dimensions.

When cultivating intimacy, you realize you do not need to rush to read every scripture verse. You can meditate on a few verses or a chapter for as long as you and God desire to communicate about them before moving on.

Unveiling Yourself to Him

Yes, God knew you before you were even formed in your mother's womb. Yes, He knows you infinitely better than you know yourself. As a result, it becomes easy to think, "Well, you already know what I'm thinking Lord, and you already know what's in my heart" and allow that to create a barrier to authentic intimacy, but intimacy requires your transparency and vulnerability.

God desires that, and whether or not you realize it, you deeply desire it as well because you have been pre-wired for fellowship with your Creator and Lover of your soul.

He's interested in hearing the cries of your heart, your frustrations, your thoughts, your gratitude, all of it! He loves you without conditions, and there is so much healing and freedom to be found in allowing God into your innermost thoughts and expressing yourself wholeheartedly, without fear, to Him.

I like how author Dr. Bruce Wilkinson said it: "God wants to hear your requests, your worries, and thanks. Risk being honest, and expect his insight in return."

What I've found is that when I am vulnerable with God, He is so faithful to remind me of the truth of who I am and how He sees me. Holy Spirit is a comforter, and a teacher, who brings me in remembrance of the words of Jesus and my heavenly Father. He reminds me that I am accepted and His beloved daughter. He picks me up off on the floor and reminds me that I am more than a conqueror through Him, yet He will speak to me in a language that is just right for me. He will do the same for you.

Practicing an active awareness of His presence

It took me years to understand what "praying without ceasing" (1 Thessalonians 5:16-18) looked like. At first, it seems like an impossibility. How can someone pray all day?

However, when you've cultivated intimacy with God, you realize it's not only praying in the more traditional sense but also having a heart attitude of prayer. A heart attitude is an awareness of His presence, a sensitivity to the leading of Holy Spirit, and ongoing communication through your words, thoughts, and actions.

The presence of God is with you always, but it is important to cultivate an active awareness of Him in your own life and business. How do you do that? By seeking Him sincerely and expecting Him to reveal himself in the mighty way that He does. I often ask God "What's your perspective on this situation?" and ask Him to help me see things from His point of view. You can ask Him for His thoughts on decisions you need to make; not just big decisions, but small ones too.

The more you engage Him in your activities, the more opportunities you create to hear and discern His voice. Take moments to pause and meditate on His goodness and thank Him for being with you as you work. It may feel unusual to you at times, but as you cultivate greater intimacy, it eventually becomes as normal as breathing.

I like the way my friend Matt Tommey, a mentor to Christian artists, says it: "The Holy Spirit wants to attune your heart and your spirit so you will be connected with Him in such a way that as He moves, breathes, and shows you things, you can respond to and move with Him in a very natural way."[1]

No formulas and no boxes

Entrepreneurs love formulas and blueprints, but I want to be clear that I am not suggesting that there is a three-step formula for cultivating intimacy with God. Cultivating intimacy is more organic than it is chronological. Additionally, God does not fit in any boxes. Cultivating intimacy with Him is not limited to one way of engagement.

Many believe that the only way to grow in intimacy with God is through reading the Bible. Acquiring knowledge through the scriptures is a vital part of our spiritual life, but knowledge without intimacy does not create a Holy Spirit-led lifestyle.

Others believe that keeping company with Jesus and having encounters with Him is the only way to grow in intimacy with God. Without meditating on the scriptures that reveal God's character, promises, and provide instruction for Kingdom living, you can easily be deceived.

> *"You search the Scriptures because you think that in them you have eternal life; and it is they that bear witness about me, yet you refuse to come to me that you may have life."*
> —John 5:39-40

> *"For the word of God is living and active, sharper than any two-edged sword, piercing to the division of soul and of spirit, of joints and of marrow, and discerning the thoughts and intentions of the heart."*
> —Hebrews 4:12

It is not about one way versus another way. Embrace the fullness of intimacy with God by breaking any boxes you may be containing Him in.

Upgrading your Intimacy with God

Life as a Kingdom Driven Entrepreneur is quite an adventure, and there is no better way to live it than through a daily companionship with Him. No matter how you would describe the quality of relationship and current level of intimacy with God, as long as you are living on this side of Heaven, there is always an upgrade available for you. Take a moment and consider the ways that you currently connect with God.

Whether you feel satisfied with your level of intimacy or not, I want to encourage you to do something new. If reading the Bible is your primary way of connecting to the Father, Jesus, and Holy Spirit, commit to spending a certain number of days to just hang out with God, rest quietly in His presence, and have conversations with Him throughout your day. Ask Him to reveal another aspect of Himself to you.

If you are not reading your Bible on a regular basis, develop a hunger for God's Word by asking God where you should start in His Word, and then start there! As you are reading, ask Holy Spirit to illuminate the scripture verses, bring them to life, and give you greater understanding.

In other words, engage with God as you read His Word. He will speak to you through it!

If you typically read the Bible without stopping to meditate on the words you are reading, begin focusing on a few scripture verses at a time and digging deeper. If you've never experienced the discipline of giving God the first fruit of your day, start waking up earlier in the morning and dedicating time to pray, worship, submit your business plans to Him and seek Him for strategy and His unique blueprints.

If you have never expressed your heart to God through journaling, grab a pen and a notebook and give it a try. If you feel like you're in a religious rut with a dry morning devotional routine, change the routine! Find a fresh way of engaging with God. Switch things up!

Intimacy through Community

We have mostly focused on what you can do while you are alone to mature in intimacy with God, yet fellowship with other believers who love God and are pursuing Him with all of their hearts has been the catalyst for some of my most significant upgrades in intimacy. I have witnessed this same dynamic in the lives of many entrepreneurs in our Igniters Mentoring Program and community. God speaks to me about fire quite a bit, so bear with me as I explain this concept of intimacy through community with a fiery analogy.

When you study fire, you learn that there are three necessary components for fire ignition and combustion (burning): a source of heat, air to supply oxygen, and fuel which can be any type of combustible material (solid, liquid, and gas).

In order for a fire to not only ignite but to continue to burn, it must have all three of these components. Any firefighter will tell you that if you remove one of these components, the fire can be contained and then extinguished.

Think of your relationship, or sonship, with God to be a flame that is ignited in your soul. If you want that fire to thrive—to never be contained or extinguished—it needs both oxygen and fuel.

Oxygen is a life-giving and life-enabling gas. It enables your ability to breathe; to inhale and exhale. Holy Spirit, or the Spirit of God, is your oxygen. The words commonly used in scripture referring to Holy Spirit are *ruach* (Hebrew) and *pneuma* (Greek) which mean wind, breath (of life), or spirit.

Now you need your fuel. You can make a legitimate case for a variety of different things serving as the fuel for maintaining a burning fire, but I wholeheartedly believe that the most powerful combustible material is other Holy Spirit-filled believers, for two primary reasons:

#1: God's design is community

God consistently shows us that we experience His best in the context of community. Consider this: God is a community all by Himself - one God, three Persons! In the beginning, He proclaimed that it was not good for man to be alone and He created community for man in the garden. When it comes to God's point of view, everything is better when community is exalted over individualism.

#2: Intimacy cultivated in community has greater Kingdom Impact

Intimacy with God is not only for the benefit of your personal relationship with your Creator. Intimacy with God should create an overflow that pours out to the people around you and has eternal Kingdom impact. We want our flames igniting one another so that the fire intensifies and spreads. That means even more people drawn into greater intimacy with the Father, Jesus Christ, and Holy Spirit.

In other words, we do not only want to have raging personal fires; we also want wildfires that spread due to all that flammable material!

That is the power of authentic Christ-centered community.

28

REFLECTION QUESTIONS

1. How are you cultivating intimacy with God?

2. In what ways can you upgrade your intimacy with God?

Reference:

1. Tommey, Matt. (2017) *Created to Thrive: An Artist's Guide to Living in Divine Abundance* [Kindle edition]

3

SUCCESS IN THE KINGDOM

"Study this Book of Instruction continually. Meditate on it day and night so you will be sure to obey everything written in it. Only then will you prosper and succeed in all you do. This is my command—be strong and courageous! Do not be afraid or discouraged. For the Lord your God is with you wherever you go."

—Joshua 1:8-9 NLT

The path to success in the Kingdom of God is not the same path that is modeled and exalted in the world. Similarly, the evidence (or proof) of success in the Kingdom of God is not the same as the evidence of success in the world.

As a Kingdom Driven Entrepreneur with a business that is yielded to God as the Ultimate CEO and led by Holy Spirit, it is important to recognize that success is not found in following the blueprint of someone else's prospering business. It is not found in following industry experts' advice in business growth. Your success is found in operating your business in both faith and obedience to God, empowered by Holy Spirit and motivated by love. Your success is found in seeking first the Kingdom of God and His righteousness.

As entrepreneurs, we love success formulas, don't we? We will invest hundreds, thousands, and even tens of thousands to learn the success formulas of the gurus and industry experts. Here is one that I believe is the most powerful one to live and work by as a Kingdom Driven Entrepreneur:

Radical Faith + Radical Obedience = Success

How can you apply this Kingdom success principle to your business? Let's explore each of these concepts.

RADICAL FAITH

Radical faith is radical trust and belief in God, leaning fully and completely into His character and resting in His promises despite what things around you may look like. Radical faith is coming into agreement with Heaven's realities rather than exalting natural circumstances.

This is the life that the King of kings modeled for us on the earth.

Radical faith is not misguided foolishness. Radical faith does not mean casting everything aside for the sake of the Gospel without any wisdom or instruction from Holy Spirit. In fact, Proverbs 1:7 says that it is a fool who despises wisdom and instruction. Jesus Christ was never foolish. He wasn't a reckless lone ranger.

In John 5:19 Jesus explained, "I tell you the truth, the Son can do nothing by himself. He does only what he sees the Father doing. Whatever the Father does, the Son also does." Jesus leaned into the truth of the Father's character.

Radical faith activates Heaven's response. It is strengthened through intimacy. As your faith increases, so do your expectations to see God move. You will be in awe when He answers prayers or when signs, wonders, and miracles follow you as you're doing the work God placed on your heart to do.

Cultivating Radical Faith

Because faith is strengthened through intimacy, many of the same ways that you cultivate intimacy are the same ways that you cultivate radical faith. For example, meditating, studying, hearing, and praying the Word of God.

Romans 10:17 says that faith comes by hearing and hearing by the Word of God.

There are additional keys to cultivating radical faith, including taking faith-filled action and persevering through trials with joy.

Taking faith-filled action

> *"Was not Abraham our father justified by works when he offered up his son Isaac on the altar? You see that faith was active along with his works, and faith was completed by his works; and the Scripture was fulfilled that says, "Abraham believed God, and it was counted to him as righteousness"—and he was called a friend of God. You see that a person is justified by works and not by faith alone."*
> —James 2:21-24

Radical faith is not truly faith unless it has a corresponding action. It is your Holy Spirit-led and empowered actions that make your faith a reality. There are three key problems that many Kingdom Driven Entrepreneurs face when it comes to taking action in business:

- Sitting idle due to fear
- Sitting idle due to complacency
- Taking faithless action instead of being led by God

You may be dealing with one of these issues knowingly or unknowingly. You may have dealt with all of them, but at different times in your entrepreneurial journey. The best news is that you have an awesome and limitless God that desires to be involved intimately in your business as your top advisor, master strategist, and business partner.

Holy Spirit is your guide to identifying and walking out your Kingdom-driven actions.

Ideas alone (even God-inspired ones) do not bring success. Implementation of those ideas is what brings success. You simply cannot afford to be idle when it comes to your business.

Casting Down the Fear

Oftentimes, we get in our own way because we have doubts and fears. We look at our circumstances and use our natural, logical reasoning and give them more credence than what the Word of God says. Believe the Word of God, which tells you, "I can do all things through Christ which strengthens me" (Philippians 4:13) and that He "has not given you a spirit of fear and timidity, but of power, love, and self-discipline" (2 Timothy 1:7).

Don't sit around waiting for things to be perfect before you take a step out and do what God has called you to do with your business. When you are bold enough to take action, God is right there with you. Resist the urge to say "You're waiting on the Lord" when He is actually waiting on you to do something. One of the best ways to tackle fear is to take action, even if it's just a small step. One small step after the other will help you gain confidence and momentum.

Resisting Complacency

Complacency (contented self-satisfaction) is a tool of the enemy, and it can impact Kingdom Driven Entrepreneurs at any experience or profitability level. The time to be most aware of this is when your business has achieved what you consider to be a "comfortable" level of success, financial or otherwise. It's sneaky because it starts off as a great feeling, but eventually, you find yourself stagnated, bored, or unmotivated. Until you have achieved the vision God has for you and your business, you must resist being lulled to sleep.

There are people in the world who need you and are waiting for you on the other side of your diligence and faithful obedience!

Find yourself faced with complacency? Pull out that notebook or journal and spend time with God to re-ignite the vision. Review your progress over the months or years and give God thanks for it all. Ask Holy Spirit to remind you of the big picture and guide you in the next steps to get moving again.

Taking God-inspired action

I rarely meet an entrepreneur who is not an action taker. It's the nature of most business owners to work diligently to see a vision come to fruition and grow in both profitability and impact. The problem is that taking action and taking faith-filled, God-inspired action are two entirely different things. The difference is important to understand because it impacts your success as a Kingdom Driven Entrepreneur.

I am all too familiar with this from my own journey. Years ago, when I left a thriving corporate career, in obedience to God, to become a full-time entrepreneur, I immediately entered what I call my "six month season of faithless action." Here is what faithless action in business looks like:

#1: Relying on your own wisdom and your own strength, working as hard as you can to make things happen in your business (also known as "the grind").

#2: Failing to seek God concerning His heart, thoughts, and plans for your business and simply submitting your own plans and asking Him to bless them. This accompanies the behavior of #1 above.

#3: Chasing after every new idea to make money any way you can. Looking to see what others have done and modeling your business activities based on what you see.

#4: Ignoring Holy Spirit's nudges to take action in an area that is uncomfortable or unfamiliar to you, and taking action based on what is convenient and within your comfort zone instead.

I distinctly remember the day in the fall of 2010 when I heard God speak to my heart and say, "Are you done yet?" after six months of grinding faithlessly in my own strength. That was the beginning of my adventure to be led by Him in my business and to eventually learn (a few years later) what it looks like to work in the unforced rhythms of His amazing grace.

Faith and corresponding action must work together in your life as a Kingdom Driven Entrepreneur. Seek God concerning your business plans, take steps in faith towards what He places on your heart (no matter how intimidating it may feel), and be willing to pivot when you receive a course correction. It's through your willingness to take action that your faith remains active and effective.

Persevering through challenges with joy

"Consider it pure joy, my brothers and sisters, whenever you face trials of many kinds, because you know that the testing of your faith produces perseverance. Let perseverance finish its work so that you may be

mature and complete, not lacking anything."
—James 1:2-4 NIV

Entrepreneurship is filled with hills and valleys; deep challenges and fulfilling triumphs. There are times you will experience a true test of your faith, and it is in those tests that radical faith increases.

In my own journey since starting the Kingdom Driven Entrepreneur movement, I faced financial loss after ceasing my previous business activities to be obedient and focus on the assignment. I experienced the unexpected loss of my co-founder Antonina when God called for her to transition out of the operations to enter her new season. I was so lost after she left that I had to take a short hiatus to mourn, allow God to heal my heart, and seek Him for direction for the next season.

I know what it's like to be diligent, faithful, and obedient in my work, yet have $10 in my bank account that needs to cover both groceries for the family and gas for the car. My family had to sell our personal home to avoid foreclosure, and we moved four times within the next three years before we were able to get settled again.

We had to say "no" to many things we used to say "yes" to. I truly had to learn how to stay both faithful and patient as we were in the early stages. Growth was slow, but it was always steady, and I remained encouraged by the impact that we were having in the lives of Kingdom business owners around the world.

While it was a challenging wilderness season, it was also filled with many moments where my family saw the miraculous provision of God and our faith was strengthened in so many ways as a result. I learned how to live in the sufficiency of God's grace on a daily basis. I still had joy and peace (most days) in the midst of it all. I got to know Jehovah Jireh intimately, the One who sees, goes before, and makes provision available.

As I was writing *Grace Over Grind: How Grace Will Take Your Business Where Grinding Can't*, God spoke to my heart that things were going to accelerate rapidly after I released the book. He said, "When you release this book, you will be the poster child for the message in it."

True to His word, after the book was released, Kingdom Driven LLC experienced unusual favor and exponential growth. Any area of the business that we measure experienced either incremental or, in most cases, exponential growth.

All of this was during the season that I had only 10-15 hours available to work each week due to caring for our newborn daughter. God began to restore what my family had lost. In fact, He's still restoring, and His kind of restoration is better than the original! I do not share my testimony to indicate that my testimony is (or even should be) the testimony of a Kingdom Driven Entrepreneur.

Your journey does not need to look like mine. I am not

saying that you have to quit a lucrative career without replacing the income first, experience dramatic income loss, sell your home, or anything like that.

What I am saying is that God still creates something beautiful out of whatever trials or challenges you experience as you place your trust in Him. Enduring through trials matures you (spiritually and naturally), reveals more of the nature of God, and increases your faith.

Are you experiencing challenges in your business? Don't be quick to walk away (unless that is what Holy Spirit instructed you to do); lean into God through the trial. Be consistent in prayer, focus, and faith-filled action. The power twins of faith and patience will usher you into the manifestation of the promises of God.

RADICAL OBEDIENCE

"But He said 'Blessed rather are those
who hear the word of God and keep it!'"
—Luke 11:28

Radical obedience is what I like to call a "lifestyle of yes." It says "yes" even when the instructions do not make sense to you or stretch you far outside of your comfort zone. It doesn't say "Yes Lord, but not right now" when He is clearly telling you to move. It says:

"Lord, that sounds absolutely ludicrous, but
Yes, Lord I'll do that."

"Lord, I have no idea how I'm going to do that,
but Yes, Lord, I trust You, and I will take the
first/next step."

"Lord, the timing for that seems a little odd,
but ok...You say now? Yes, let's do it."

Placing yourself and your business under subjection to God
is a daily decision. It is a decision to yield to His ways and
be led by His word and His Spirit. What happens when you
sense God leading you to stop when you're in the middle of
an important project with an impending deadline in order to
make a phone call and pray with someone He places on your
heart? What if you get an email inviting you to be a guest on
a show that you have been dreaming of being on, but you
feel a strong "No, not yet" from Holy Spirit?

Being faithful in moments like these takes submission,
knowing that God is fully aware of your deadlines and desires.
I've found in my own life that embracing this daily surrender
creates fun adventures with God and opportunities to see how
very involved and interested He is in my business.

Pastor and speaker Bob Sorge describes radical obedience
as "immediate obedience that fulfills the commandment to
its fullest measure; it does not seek to comply to the minimal

standards but pursues extravagant, lavish fulfillment."[1]

Extravagant and lavish fulfillment—that is God's best. It is what you, as a Kingdom Driven Entrepreneur, should position yourself to receive through your willingness to hear and immediately respond.

The Bible provides a number of examples where radical faith and obedience yielded supernatural success—stories of Moses, Abraham, Nehemiah, David, Queen Esther, Shadrach, Meshach, and Abednego, Peter and so many others. One of the most notable stories is when God instructed Joshua to lead his men around the walls of Jericho once a day for six days, and then on the seventh day to march around the wall seven times with the priests blowing horns.

He said, "It shall come to pass, when they make a long *blast* with the ram's horn, *and* when you hear the sound of the trumpet, that all the people shall shout with a great shout; then the wall of the city will fall down flat."

In faith, Joshua was obedient to God's instruction and found success when the wall of the city fell just as God said it would. Not only did Joshua prosper, but the people of Israel prospered under his leadership (Joshua 6:1-5).

Jesus Christ's life was the epitome of radical obedience— He faced testing in the wilderness with Satan, He remained obedient to His Father during His time on earth by doing only what He saw his Father do, and He ultimately suffered and humbly died on the cross. He was obedient to the point of death (Philippians 2:8)!

You know the story, but His obedience unto death became life as He rose again. The blessing through His obedience is that we have been reconciled back to God, and those who dare to believe can experience an abundant life in Him on earth and for eternity. His obedience made the Kingdom of God a reality!

The pages you are reading in this book right now are a fruit of radical obedience. If Antonina Geer and I had failed to say 'yes' to launching the Kingdom Driven Entrepreneur movement in 2012, this book never would have been written.

You may not know this, but when God gave us the assignment of starting Kingdom Driven Entrepreneur, I did not know what a Kingdom Driven Entrepreneur was.

I knew what it meant to be a Christian operating business in integrity, but not as one who is Kingdom-minded and Kingdom-focused for Kingdom impact in the marketplace. We had to sit at the feet of Jesus and learn.

After six months of on-the-job training with Jesus, Kingdom Driven LLC was formally created, and a movement was birthed. We did not have 10,000 hours of expertise or years of revelatory wisdom that had been applied in our own businesses, yet God called us to launch anyway. He didn't call us to lead a guru movement, but rather a yielded one. We had to walk the journey out in real time in front of others. We had to share the challenges and breakthroughs along the way. We had to make mistakes in front of an audience.

We chose to be radically obedient because we were

compelled by love and we wanted to experience the "extravagant, lavish fulfillment" of whatever was on His heart.

Cultivating Radical Obedience

"If you fully obey the Lord your God and carefully follow all his commands I give you today, the Lord your God will set you high above all the nations on earth. All these blessings will come on you and accompany you if you obey the Lord your God."
—Deuteronomy 28:1-2 NIV

The glory of God is revealed as you follow the guidance of Holy Spirit in your business through your daily operations and strategic decision making as a Kingdom Driven Entrepreneur. Your obedience unlocks Heaven's resources and brings a manifestation of God's blessing.

Your obedience has ripple effects that impact the lives of many. Through your radical obedience, you will experience the miraculous move of God through your business that will astound you and others in your sphere of influence.

Hear and then do

"Do not merely listen to the word, and so deceive yourselves. Do what it says. [Whoever]

looks intently into the perfect law that gives freedom, and continues in it—not forgetting what they have heard, but doing it—they will be blessed in what they do."

—James 1:22, 25 NIV

In order to be radically obedient, you have to abide in Christ and hear the voice of God by His Spirit. Radical obedience requires first hearing in order to respond and do. You can access the voice of God through reading the Bible, and thanks to Holy Spirit you can access specific guidance and instructions in the moment wherever you are. You can receive guidance and wisdom for business decisions and interactions with others you encounter in the marketplace.

Whether you believe it or not, you have the ability to hear His voice. Jesus Christ, the King of kings, said, "My sheep hear my voice, and I know them, and they follow me."

Notice He did not say His sheep *might* hear His voice or *can* hear His voice. He said His sheep *will* hear His voice (John 10:27).

There have been quite a few times that God gave me a specific direction that seemed illogical. As mentioned earlier, the Kingdom Driven Entrepreneur movement started from a decision to be radically obedient to instructions that made no earthly sense. That was only the beginning of the journey, to say yes to unusual directions.

In 2013, we decided to plan a retreat for the community

and to say it was an interesting experience is an understatement. We put together a schedule and attempted to create an agenda, but when we were seeking God about what He had on His heart for the agenda, He would only give us instructions on the logistics without any insight on the content.

We had questions! "How are we going to prepare for them, Lord? Don't we need to create some charts or something? What are we doing? What do you want us to teach about?" Multiple times in the middle of prayer, God gave me visions about the retreat, but when I asked the Lord to help me to understand the details of what was happening in those brief encounters so that we could create an agenda, He still wanted to talk about logistics, but no content! Whenever Antonina would seek the Lord about the agenda, He'd simply tell her not to worry about it because the attendees were coming to encounter Him.

The fruit of our obedience to give Him full control over the agenda within our planned schedule was a business retreat with close to 40 people that can only be described as a radical encounter with God. His manifested presence met us that weekend. People were healed emotionally, delivered, restored, affirmed, and re-positioned for what God called them to do in the marketplace.

For me, a redeemed control freak and meticulous planner, it was a necessary stretch that deepened my relationship with Abba and increased my faith in His character. Since that time, I have received unusual instructions on how to price some of our products and services. I have humbled myself to be responsive to His leading and ask for help from others in ways that on the surface seemed unwise (and were certainly out of my comfort zone). In any situation I have faced in business that called for radical obedience, when I dared to respond accordingly, I truly experienced God's best.

Jesus said, "Father, if it is your will, take this cup away from me; nevertheless not my will, but yours, be done." That is the heart of a Kingdom Driven Entrepreneur. Yield your plans to Him. Exchange them for His best. You will not be left disappointed.

Expect Greater Clarity as You Move

> *"The heart of a man plans his way, but the Lord establishes his steps."*
> *"The steps of a man are established by the Lord, when he delights in his way."*
> —Proverbs 16:9; Psalm 37:23

One of the challenges a Kingdom Driven Entrepreneur faces when choosing to live a "lifestyle of yes" is the desire to have perfect clarity on everything before taking a step because the risk of getting something inspired by God wrong feels too great. If that is you, I want you to lean in and read this carefully:

That is not how this works.

Obedience in the small things often unlocks the next step, then the next step, until it begins to reveal a much larger and clearer picture. That is part of what makes obedience radical - responding to God without all of the details! The pursuit for clarity prior to operating in obedience will stagnate your progress because clarity often comes in your movement.

You have to embrace the mystery of the journey. You will only see in part, and you will only see as much as God desires to show you as you lean into Him. Your plans should be held loosely. Your Ultimate CEO knows best.

Let me illustrate this with a story about the first year of Kingdom Driven LLC. Antonina and I started with one instruction we had from God, which was *"Kingdom Driven Entrepreneur is a community, a movement, and it starts with a book."* That was enough to get started, but very quickly there were other questions that needed to be answered. *What's the book about? How do we start the community?*

Once we got past those hurdles, we had more questions. *Now that there is an online community here, what are we supposed to do with them?* We felt like God had given us a vision to make Jesus Christ known in the marketplace globally, but the "how" was not clear.

Sure, we could teach the little bit that we had in our first book, but in our minds, that did not feel like enough. We wanted to serve these 2,000 people who showed up enthusiastically wanting more about doing Kingdom business.

More questions arose: "God, we believe you led this to

be a for-profit structure, so we're supposed to generate revenue. How?" We did our best to prayerfully come up with a mission for how we accomplish the vision God gave us. Our first mission was "To equip entrepreneurs of faith to build thriving businesses so they can serve their families, truly impact lives, and advance the Kingdom of God."

With that mission in mind and a Facebook community with a few thousand people asking a lot of questions about the nuts and bolts of doing business, we found it easy to teach concepts around building a Kingdom driven business and creating virtual events with other Christians who were experts in various areas of business-building.

Trust me when I say that it was much easier to focus on teaching people the nuts and bolts of business-building because current and aspiring entrepreneurs pay to learn those things. It was hard for us (at the time) to reconcile the idea of selling a product or service (beyond books) that taught the principles of doing business led by Holy Spirit.

The community was growing, and we were serving as best as we knew how. We were teaching principles on how to do business God's way for free via podcast teachings, interviews, and sharing in our free online community. We were also offering paid programs that helped entrepreneurs grow their businesses using the skills that we had learned over the years in our own businesses prior to launching the Kingdom Driven Entrepreneur movement.

We collaborated with others to fill in skills gaps that we

could not offer ourselves so that the community could benefit from our collective experience. We also published a number of books on topics such as Kingdom driven goal setting, leadership, and business finances.

After operating this way for ten months, we experienced our first significant course correction. We had just finished plans for our third online event; a virtual conference called Break the Chains: Systems for Business Success. We had all of the pieces in place, and we were excited to share it and help our community. We also anticipated that it would be our most profitable offering since we launched. With our previous two free online events we had several hundred sign-ups, but with this particular virtual conference, we had only three people register and purchase a ticket.

We were stunned, but the message was abundantly clear: we needed to make a shift. We had no idea what that meant or what it looked like, so we decided to fast and pray until we knew what to do next. A few days into the fast, I was in my closet praying, and God spoke to my heart about fire. He told me that fire represented His power, presence, passion, and purity, and directed me to the scriptures to study it more.

It was in those moments that the mission shifted for Kingdom Driven Entrepreneur. I heard the words, "You are activating Firestarters in the marketplace."

It was clear that our assignment was not to teach the nuts and bolts of business-building, but to solely focus on shifting the mindsets and heart posture of believers and show what it looks like to truly be Kingdom-driven in business and led by Holy Spirit. The clarity came as we moved in obedience to what God had already revealed.

He kept some things hidden for us when we first started because we needed to lean into Him and pursue Him with all of our hearts to discover them. We learned so much in that first year, and even as we were learning and sorting out more of the details of what our assignment was, we were able to have a positive impact on the lives and businesses of several hundred entrepreneurs

Expect to move without all the details. God is faithful to keep you from veering too far from the path as you continue to keep your eyes, ears, and mostly your heart attuned to knowing more of His plan. Radical faith and radical obedience is the lifestyle of a Kingdom Driven Entrepreneur and the key to success in Kingdom business.

That does not mean that the journey is always going to be easy, but it is the Holy Spirit-led lifestyle that will take your business from one level of glory to the next.

REFLECTION QUESTIONS

1. Are you taking faith-filled and Holy Spirit-led action in your business? If not, what will be your next step to shift how you work? Ask Holy Spirit for help.

2. What instructions has God given you in your business that you have not yet been obedient to follow?

3. What does a "lifestyle of yes" look like to you personally?

Reference:

1. Sorge, Bob. "The Secret of Radical Obedience." Christianity Today, 4 Jan. 2006, www.christianitytoday.com/biblestudies/articles/theology/060104.html.

4

ASSETS IN HEAVEN'S ECONOMY

"The Lord will open to you his good treasury, the heavens, to give the rain to your land in its season and to bless all the work of your hands."

—Deuteronomy 28:12

The economics of the world are vastly different from the economics of Heaven. As a Kingdom Driven Entrepreneur, you have access to the unlimited supply of Heaven to provide everything that you need to do what God has called you to do.

Too often we fall into the trap of self-sufficiency due to our God-given ability to thoroughly and independently perform research. We also allow our own (or others') experiences and circumstances to shape our understanding or belief in what is possible and miss out on God's best. 2 Corinthians 9:8 states:

"And God is able to make all grace abound toward you, that you, always having all sufficiency in all things, may have an abundance for every good work."

This "sufficiency in all things" and "abundance for every good work" is not obtained in your own strength. That mindset limits you to the world's economic system and the world's blueprints.

As a Kingdom Driven Entrepreneur, you only want to be self-sufficient in Christ's sufficiency. Heaven's economy beats the world's economy every single time. Heavenly assets, when stewarded well, will unlock tremendous levels of growth and increase your Kingdom impact in ways beyond your imagination.

Investopedia.com defines an asset as a resource with economic value that an individual, corporation, or country owns or controls with the expectation that it will provide a future benefit. Simply stated, assets represent value of ownership that can be converted into cash.

When it comes to the heavenly assets, I submit the following revised definition for your consideration: a resource with economic value that a Kingdom Driven Entrepreneur stewards with the expectation that it will provide a future benefit. Heavenly assets represent an eternal value that can be converted into a manifestation of blessing (for the benefit of the entrepreneur and those within his/her sphere of influence).

Before we discuss some of the heavenly assets available to you as a Kingdom Driven Entrepreneur, it is important to set the proper foundation. Abba, your heavenly Father, is the source of the unlimited supply. He is God. He is the Source, and everything else is a resource. There is no other, and there is no one else like Him. Every heavenly asset in His economy is timeless because He is eternal.

In the Kingdom of God, Jesus Christ is King and is Lord over time. He was with God in the beginning. He created all things and sustains all things. He is the first and the last, the beginning and the end, the One who is, was, and is to come. He is the same yesterday, today, and forever.

It is easy to forget that God is the Source and instead focus on the resources, both natural and supernatural. The resources are nothing without the Source. Hold that truth in your heart while we explore the assets Heaven has made available to you to do business in the Kingdom of God.

1. Knowledge, Understanding, and Wisdom

Three of Heaven's greatest assets available to you are knowledge, understanding, and wisdom.

Although many people use these terms interchangeably, they are different. Knowledge is information and facts, understanding is the ability to give meaning to that knowledge, and wisdom is knowing what to do with (how to properly apply) that knowledge. Knowledge, understanding, and wisdom are God's gifts to you and are vital for Kingdom life.

The Bible is full of confirmation of this, but here are a few to meditate on:

> *"For the Lord gives wisdom; from his*
> *mouth come knowledge and understanding;*
> *He stores up sound wisdom for the upright;*
> *He is a shield to those who walk in integrity."*
> —Proverbs 2:6-7

> *"My people are destroyed for lack*
> *of knowledge."*
> —Hosea 4:6

> *"An intelligent heart acquires knowledge,*
> *and the ear of the wise seeks knowledge."*
> —Proverbs 18:15

> *"Understanding is a wellspring*
> *of life to him who has it."*
> —Proverbs 16:22 NKJV

> *"Wisdom is the principal thing; Therefore*
> *get wisdom. And in all your getting, get*
> *understanding."*
> —Proverbs 4:7 NKJV

I'll illustrate the difference with a simple, yet life-changing example from my own entrepreneurial journey. I'd heard and read Matthew 11:28-30 in the Bible numerous times throughout my life. Jesus Christ proclaimed that His yoke was easy and that His burden was light.

I knew (and believed) this fact, but it was purely head knowledge. Then, I experienced an illumination in my heart—a supernatural moment of insight—when hearing a different translation of the verse during a sermon at my local church. It was The Message translation, and it said: "Are you tired? Worn out? Burned out on religion? Come to me. Get away with me and you'll recover your life. I'll show you how to take a real rest. Walk with me and work with me—watch how I do it. Learn the unforced rhythms of grace. I won't lay anything heavy or ill-fitting on you. Keep company with me and you'll learn to live freely and lightly."

Suddenly, the knowledge I had became understanding. The lights were turned on by the power of Holy Spirit, and I was able to really give these verses meaning in the context of entrepreneurship. Before starting Kingdom Driven LLC, my entrepreneurial lifestyle was one of the hustle and grind.

The Kingdom Driven Entrepreneur movement was birthed with the knowledge and understanding of God's grace in business, and it eventually grew exponentially in influence, impact, and income by the wisdom that Holy Spirit provided on how to practically apply that knowledge and understanding.

Proverbs 24:3-4 ties it all together beautifully:

Through wisdom a house is built,
and by understanding it is established;
by knowledge the rooms are filled with all
precious and pleasant riches."

Wisdom, understanding, and knowledge will work together to cause the business that God has placed on your heart to thrive. The wisdom of God is required to build it, understanding provides a secure foundation for it, and knowledge is the critical seed to ensure that you and your business has what is needed to accomplish the goodness the business was created for.

A Kingdom Driven Entrepreneur never needs to chase dollars. When you serve faithfully, God will increase your business through the heavenly assets of godly knowledge, understanding, and wisdom.

2. Kingdom Math

When you are operating your business according to Heaven's economics, you quickly realize that you are not limited by the rules of basic mathematics you learned as a child. With Kingdom math, five loaves of bread and two fish feed over 5,000 people...and there are still leftovers (Matthew 14:13-21)! With Kingdom math, you can take one jar of oil and have it fill (to the brim) every empty vessel you can get your hands on (2 Kings 4:1-7).

In other words, God can and will multiply what little you have and produce something extraordinary when it is yielded to Him and aligned with His purpose. Heaven has an unlimited supply because God Himself and King Jesus are unlimited. When God breathes on what you are doing, you can expect to be astounded!

Kingdom math is not an asset that is focused solely on the multiplication of material things, but it can also mean time multiplication (supernatural productivity), talent and gifts multiplication, or multiplication of any other spiritual or natural resource. I have personally seen the power of Kingdom math in action in these first six years of Kingdom Driven LLC and the Kingdom Driven Entrepreneur movement.

We experienced our greatest growth (exponential growth!) during a season that I had the least amount of time to work. I have seen God take my little bit of money I had to invest in something He placed on my heart to do and increase it to exactly what was needed. I have seen God replace and grow our income in times when we were radically generous to take our little "widow's mite" and sow it into helping someone else. I have seen God take my willingness to tell one short story at His leading and see that message create an atmosphere of deliverance for a room full of people.

Too often we look poorly at a circumstance where we have inadequate resources to work with, but these are times to rejoice because it is an opportunity for you and for others to see the glory of God revealed through Heaven's unlimited supply. He will supply all of your need according to His riches in glory (Philippians 4:19).

3. Spiritual Gifts

Holy Spirit living on the inside of you enables you to produce fruit. You're empowered to produce love, joy, peace, patience (long suffering), kindness, goodness, faithfulness, gentleness, and self-control. This is clearly important for doing business God's way.

Additionally, you've been empowered by Holy Spirit with specific spiritual gifts that will not only help you be exponentially more effective at the work you do in your business, but also serve as a way to advance the Kingdom of God.

Through your spiritual gifts, you can be a demonstrator of God's presence, power, and love to prospects, customers, clients, employees, vendors, or anyone else you encounter through the work that you do. These gifts are distributed to individual members of the body of Christ as He wills and are given for the benefit of all. These gifts should be motivated by authentic love and a desire to see the glory of God revealed.

All gifts should be honored, and one should not be exalted more than the others. The Bible mentions a variety of spiritual gifts of Holy Spirit in Romans 12, 1 Corinthians 12, and Ephesians 4.

Romans 12:6-8 gifts: prophecy, service, giving, teaching, exhortation, leadership, mercy

1 Corinthians 12:8-10, 28-30 gifts: word of wisdom, word of knowledge, healing, miracles, prophecy, discerning of spirits, speaking in tongues, interpretation of tongues, faith, helps, administration, apostle, prophet, teacher

Ephesians 4:11-12 gifts: the roles of apostle, prophet, evangelist, pastor, and teacher for the equipping of God's people for ministry (service)

As the host of The Kingdom Driven Entrepreneur Podcast, I've had the pleasure of speaking with entrepreneurs around the world about their journey of doing business in partnership with God. Here are a few examples of how some Kingdom Driven Entrepreneurs embraced their spiritual gifts in their work:

Word of Knowledge: A word of knowledge is information revealed to you by Holy Spirit that you otherwise wouldn't have known on your own. It can come from an inward revelation, a dream, a vision, through the Word of God, or through other means.

> *Tasha Glover*, a digital marketing agency owner, shared how God often gives her a word of knowledge (through dreams) concerning the personal life or business of a client that she is providing strategic guidance to.

> Her willingness to take the risk and share what she believes God has shown her has proven to be blessing and confirmation for her clients that are struggling with a key decision that needs to be made or has already been made.

Prophecy: Prophecy is a divinely inspired message revealing the will of God. The act of prophesying is speaking this message under the inspiration of the Holy Spirit, discerning what it is that the Lord wants to have shared at that time for a particular person or group of people. It can be predictive and can also be a speaking forth of God's Word.

A prophetic word serves to strengthen, encourage, and comfort; it can also bring conviction to those who hear it, drawing them to Christ.

> *Dr. Tony Robinson*, a prophetic advisor, coach, and strategist shared how she asks God to reveal His heart concerning every individual

she works with, and Holy Spirit consistently delivers. When she speaks the word that God gives her to her clients, it often helps those who are stuck get unstuck, brings healing to broken hearts, and draws them into a more intimate relationship with the Father.

Evangelist: Every believer is called to share the gospel, but there are also evangelists who are empowered by Holy Spirit to passionately lead people beyond their natural sphere of influence to the saving knowledge of Jesus Christ.

Jeff Jerina is a business owner and evangelist in the marketplace. In his holiday lighting design company, he has led a number of people he encounters, both contractors and customers, into a relationship with Jesus Christ. He also teaches, trains, and encourages other believers on personal evangelism and how to share the gospel effectively with the people around them as God orchestrates the opportunity to do so.

A full discussion of spiritual gifts is beyond the scope of this book, but I highly recommend Darren Shearer's *The Marketplace Christian: A Practical Guide to Using Your Spiritual Gifts in Business* to learn how to discover and then apply the gifts that God has equipped you with by the power of His Spirit.

The A.G.A.P.E. Framework for Operating in Heaven's Economy

One of my favorite songs in this season is called *Build My Life* by Housefires. There is a line that says, "And I will build my life upon your love, it is a firm foundation." The unconditional love of God is absolutely a firm foundation to build our lives on, and I believe it is also a firm foundation to build our businesses on as Kingdom Driven Entrepreneurs. With that said, I would like to offer you a framework for understanding how heavenly assets are accessed and how to operate in Heaven's economy. The acronym A.G.A.P.E. has a dual purpose—to help you remember the framework itself and to serve as a reminder that love is at the center of it all.

A: Ask

> *"Ask, and it will be given to you; seek, and you will find; knock, and it will be opened to you. For everyone who asks receives, and the one who seeks finds, and to the one who knocks it will be opened."*
>
> —Matthew 7:7-9

*"Until now you have asked nothing in my
name. Ask, and you will receive, that your
joy may be full."*
−John 16:24

The King of kings, Jesus Christ, emphasized the power of the
ask. The Apostle Paul did as well:

*"If any of you lacks wisdom, you should ask
God, who gives generously to all without find-
ing fault, and it will be given to you."*
−James 1:5 NIV

*"You do not have, because you do not ask.
You ask and do not receive, because you ask
wrongly, to spend it on your passions."*
−James 4:23

Asking, according to the will of God, will access the heavenly
assets of knowledge, understanding, and wisdom. If you lack
wisdom (anytime, anywhere, and on any business matter),
ask God, and He will reveal His wisdom by His Spirit and
through His Word.

The best news is that not only does God give you wisdom,
but He does so without finding fault in you for asking Him
(read James 1:5 for proof)!

That is not a small thing, and too many entrepreneurs

fail to tap into His wisdom when faced with a problem that requires a solution.

How many times have you not asked God for wisdom simply because you didn't want to bother Him with such small details or what you consider to be minor matters? Or maybe you think you should already know the solution to your issue and feel shame for asking. Or perhaps you just asked God for wisdom 10 minutes ago about something else, and now you don't feel like you should ask Him for wisdom again on another matter so soon.

Ask God for wisdom concerning your business! Holy Spirit may lead you to a specific scripture verse, may speak an answer to your heart, may make your path clear by removing blocks, or lead you to a specific resource or individual who will provide you with knowledge, understanding, or wisdom.

Often you will find that it is the collective wisdom, understanding, and knowledge from multiple people that leads you to solutions for your Kingdom business. For example, perhaps you have the knowledge, but the access to understanding and wisdom comes from other people and resources God places in your path.

Alternatively, you may not have all the knowledge needed, yet God will give you wisdom on how to apply the knowledge that was made available to you from others.

When you ask God for wisdom, the key is to not only ask, but to also:

- Have a willing mind and heart to receive His wisdom
- Fully commit to submitting to the wisdom you receive
- Endure patiently and faithfully as you await His answer

G: Give Generously

"There is one who scatters, yet increases more; And there is one who withholds more than is right, but it leads to poverty. The generous soul will be made rich, and he who waters will also be watered himself."
—Proverbs 11:24-25 NKJV

In Heaven's economy, when you sow sparingly, you also reap sparingly; and when you sow bountifully, you also reap bountifully. When you humbly recognize God as the one who enables you to create wealth, and you rightfully recognize your role as the steward of the wealth that God owns, it's easy to honor Him with your finances and embrace intentional radical generosity.

Regardless of your current level of profitability, honoring God with your increase will make the economy of Heaven available to you. I am not suggesting that you give generously solely in order to receive, but the truth of God's Word and the spiritual laws He has put in place state that when you sow a seed, you will reap a harvest, and every seed produces of its own kind (Galatians 6:7, Genesis 1:11).

As a Kingdom Driven Entrepreneur, you have to hold your material possessions loosely, personal and business finances included. They do not belong to you. In the Kingdom of God, you are not an owner. You are a steward (or manager) of what belongs to God. Your mindset should be that 100% of your income is available to God. Whatever God calls for from you, you should be obedient to release it.

Think of yourself (and your business) as a distribution center in the Kingdom of God. A distribution center is a warehouse or other building that redistributes products on demand to retailers, wholesalers, or directly to consumers. When there is an order (a demand) placed on the products, the distribution center sends them out. This is the picture of the Kingdom Driven Entrepreneur.

When God places a demand on what is in the warehouse, you send it out. Charles Spurgeon, an influential Baptist preacher from the 19th century, is quoted as saying:

> "In all of my years of service to my Lord, I have discovered a truth that has never failed and has never been compromised. That truth is that it is beyond the realm of possibilities that one has the ability to out give God. Even if I give the whole of my worth to Him, He will find a way to give back to me much more than

I gave."

That's how the economy of Heaven operates. As a Kingdom Driven Entrepreneur, you are a channel for resources (financial and otherwise) to flow to and through—so give and give generously!

A: Align

> *"For my thoughts are not your thoughts, neither are your ways my ways,' declares the Lord. For as the heavens are higher than the earth, so are my ways higher than your ways and my thoughts than your thoughts.'"*
> —Isaiah 55:8-9

Align means to be in or come into precise adjustment or correct relative position. Aligning your thoughts with God's thoughts, your words with God's words, and your actions with God's ways is key to accessing any heavenly asset.

In order to have the mind of Christ and boldly declare God's words (to yourself, to others, to your situations), you have to spend time reading and meditating on His Word.

In chapter 2, I mentioned how reading and meditating on scriptures helps you to have more intimate fellowship with Him, but it also helps you to see people, things, and circumstances through Heaven's lens.

The ways of the Kingdom begin to frame not only your perspective but also your response.

I shared the following in my book *Grace Over Grind: How Grace Will Take Your Business Where Grinding Can't:*

> It's important to renew your mind daily, and one of the ways to do that is think about what you're thinking about and align your thoughts with God's word. A great way of doing this is to use Philippians 4:8-9 as a filter.

> The scripture says, "whatever is true, whatever is noble, whatever is right, whatever is pure, whatever is lovely, whatever is admirable, if anything is excellent or praiseworthy -- think about such things."

> Take your thoughts through the filter. Does it pass? Is it true? Do your thoughts reflect God's thoughts? Sometimes you'll know the answer by getting into the scriptures and allowing Holy Spirit to illuminate the Word in your heart. Other times Holy Spirit will bring the Word to you.

If the thought doesn't pass the filters, don't go off running full steam ahead with that thought; bring it captive. Make it a prisoner and turn it over to God, asking Him to replace it with His thoughts.

Renewing your mind is not a one-time event; it is a continuous process and a progressive journey. Proverbs 4:23 instructs "Keep your heart with all diligence, for out of it spring the issues of life." The word "heart" in this scripture is *leb* in Hebrew, meaning your soul, mind, and thinking.

The word "keep" is *natsar* in Hebrew, meaning to guard and preserve. To keep your heart means to guard and preserve your mind and thinking because it will determine your actions. The more you align your thoughts, the more frequently your words and actions will also be in alignment.

When you align your thoughts, words, and actions with God concerning your business, the enemy is well aware and will seek to distract and destroy. The enemy certainly does not want you to access heavenly assets or to believe that they are available to you.

When those negative thoughts or distracting circumstances arise, you can simply stand against the lies by standing in the truth of God's Word, and the devil has to flee.

P: Praise

"Bless the LORD, O my soul; and forget not all His benefits." —Psalm 103:2

"Because your steadfast love is better than life, my lips will praise you." —Psalm 63:3

"Let everything that has breath praise the Lord. Praise the Lord!" —Psalm 150:6

God is always good. When things are going great in your business, He's good. When circumstances are frustrating, and it seems like all hell broke loose in your business, He is still good! His greatness cannot be measured. He is worthy of your praise every moment of every day in your life. The simple fact that you are able to read the pages of this book right now is enough reason to praise Him!

His worthiness is enough reason to praise Him, yet there is also tremendous power in your authentic praise that positions you to access assets in the heavenly realms. The praise you release from the very breath that God gave you can access God's promises in the unseen realm and bring them into full manifestation. When you focus your mind on God's amazing goodness and release that praise to Him, it takes your focus off of self and beholds Him, the Source.

Consider examples of how the power of God was released

through praise in the Bible:

Paul and Silas

Paul and Silas sang praises so loud to God while in prison that the other prisoners could hear them and "suddenly" there was a great earthquake that shook the very foundations of the prison. The doors flew open, their prison chains were broken, and they were released from captivity (Acts 16:16-40).

King Jehoshaphat

The Lord instructed King Jehoshaphat to put the praise team right on the front line of battle rather than the soldiers - and they were completely surrounded by a vast army of enemies! God spoke through a prophet to assure the King that He would fight the battle on his behalf, and the choir sang praises to God in the beauty of holiness, "Praise the Lord, for His mercy endures forever."

The results of their praise? Their enemies started fighting amongst themselves! The enemy was defeated, and Judah had the victory (2 Chronicles 20).

God is still the same today. If praise could release the power of God back then, praise can release the power of God now and lead to supernatural breakthrough and acceleration in your business. Praise God now for the manifestation of the vision He has given you for your business.

Understand that the work has already been finished and every resource you need has already been accounted for—human, financial, or otherwise. By praising your eternal and limitless God now, you are activating faith, supernaturally shaking your prison foundations, and releasing your destiny.

E: Embrace Unity

Seeing the glory of God revealed in the earth and expanding the Kingdom of God is not a solo pursuit, but rather a Body of Christ pursuit. It takes the body working together to fulfill the purposes of God. We are both created and called to unity with one another.

We need the creativity, the shared resources, the accountability, the strengthening, and the pure Holy Spirit outpouring that is found when Kingdom people come together on one accord with a shared purpose (remember the early church in the book of Acts). This was even the prayer of our King! Jesus lifted His eyes to the heavens and prayed to the Father:

> *"I have given them the glory that you gave me, that they may be one as we are one— I in them and you in me—so that they may be brought to complete unity. Then the world will know that you sent me and have loved them even as you have loved me."*
>
> —John 17:22-23

I shared earlier how often you will find that it is the collective wisdom, understanding, and knowledge from multiple people that leads you to solutions for your Kingdom business. There is also favor and resources of all kinds locked up in other people that God desires to connect you with in order to see His purposes fulfilled in your business.

You will be a divine connection for others, and God has divine connections specifically for you. These people are multipliers and accelerate your growth, often times exponentially.

When you embrace these connections, what would have ordinarily taken five or ten years for you to achieve on your own can be done in significantly less time because you're aligned with someone who is strategically placed in your life.

In short, embracing unity and a spirit of collaboration gives you access to Kingdom math!

These divine connections can be mentors, coaches, advisors, investors, connectors, partners, supportive friends, peers, or complete strangers. Here are a few ways that you can identify a divine connection orchestrated by God. Not all of these will necessarily apply, but at least one of them will:

The person "up-levels" your purpose or assignment.

What I mean by this is that the person takes your thinking about your vision to a new level—they add more life to it. Perhaps it is through a new idea, an expansion to your idea, or a new dimension to your vision. What that person offers will not be something that distracts or detracts from your vision; it will resonate in your spirit.

> *The person encourages you, motivates you,*
> *and simply will not allow you to quit.*

These people are genuinely excited about what God is doing in your life and business. They may not even understand the details, have any expertise in what you're doing, but their hearts are connected to yours.

> *The person actively seeks opportunities to con-*
> *nect you to resources you need to facilitate*
> *progress with your purpose or assignment.*

These people are not about "you scratch my back and I'll scratch yours." These people give from their heart and are willing to help even when there is no immediate payback for them.

Why? Because they are Kingdom minded and they are responsive to the leading of the Spirit. They are sowing into the Kingdom and know that they will reap from the Kingdom.

> *Whenever you're with this person, you sense the*
> *presence of God in the midst of your gatherings.*

Your conversations are divinely inspired—they are anointed conversations—and they are not always about business but can also just be about life. There are some people whose mere presence can activate or ignite you. You're more creative, more inspired, more on fire for the Kingdom.

The duration and depth of these connections will vary widely. Some will not develop into much of a relationship at all, but yet still accomplish God's purposes. Be sensitive to the leading of Holy Spirit because He will guide in this area and help you recognize the connection points that He is orchestrating on both yours and others' behalf. Be prepared to give of yourself and be equally prepared to receive.

REFLECTION QUESTIONS

1. In what areas do you lack knowledge, understanding, or wisdom in your business? (Action: List them all out and inquire God about each of them individually)

2. Have you experienced the power of any of the heavenly assets in your business? If so, in what ways? Your own testimonies will inspire you to go further and deeper.

3. Which concepts in the A.G.A.P.E. framework resonated the most with you, and why? How can you apply the framework to your business?

5

RE-THINKING STEWARDSHIP

"The Lord will open to you his good treasury, the heavens, to give the rain to your land in its season and to bless all the work of your hands."

—Deuteronomy 28:12

Holman Bible Dictionary defines stewardship as "Utilizing and managing all resources God provides for the glory of God and the betterment of his creations." When you think about the concept of stewardship, you likely think about time, talent, material possessions, or finances. You think about the resources that are currently within your possession and how you can better manage them faithfully.

Every Kingdom Driven Entrepreneur is called to a focus on stewardship, particularly if we desire to be entrusted with more. In the Parable of the Talents, Jesus made it clear that when we are faithful over a little, we can be trusted to be rulers over much more.

I want to re-shape your thinking about stewardship because God reshaped mine and it had a substantial impact on the productivity and progress with Kingdom Driven LLC and the Kingdom Driven Entrepreneur movement. God showed me that in order to operate effectively in Heaven's economy, stewarding the unseen is often more important than stewarding what is in my hand. Heaven's unlimited supply is available to Kingdom Driven Entrepreneurs who are completely yielded to God, working in His rest and grace instead of grinding in their own strength, and devoted to His purposes.

How are you stewarding the promises of God in your business that you haven't seen with your eyes yet?

They could be general promises made to all believers from the scripture or specific promises that God spoke personally to your heart concerning your business.

How are you stewarding a vision of something in your business that you have very little details on and inadequate finances for? How are you stewarding your time to do the uncomfortable things God has instructed you to do that do not make any sense based upon what you see? How are you stewarding the measure of faith that you have? What does stewardship of the unseen look like for you?

These questions are important to answer because if you

are not focusing on stewarding the things you cannot see, how will you get to the point where you see them? If you have a big vision for your business and you take your role in the Kingdom seriously, it will not be done by your might or power, but only by the Spirit of God.

You have to steward the unseen realm. The reality of what you do not see is greater than the reality of what you see.

Kingdom Driven LLC has a God-sized vision with substantial, unseen provision, so learning stewardship in this area and exercising my faith muscles was key to ensuring that we continued to position ourselves as an organization to access what God had for us.

I want to share with you a series of lessons that Holy Spirit taught me about stewarding the unseen because I have seen the rewards of leaning all the way into the character of God and His unlimited supply. I am committed to increasing my capacity for more of Heaven in the work that I do to reveal His glory on the earth. I pray that you are committed to the same!

Lesson #1: God can simultaneously provide for both your business and family

This probably sounds like a ridiculous thing to say because it should be obvious. Can I be real with you? It was not obvious to me, and so I have to believe that it may not be obvious to others. I had radical faith in God's ability to provide for

Kingdom Driven LLC and the Kingdom Driven Entrepreneur movement (which He did and continues to do), but I did not have faith that God would simultaneously provide for both the movement and me personally if I chose to compensate myself regularly. I was so certain that the work I was doing was all His (which it was), but somehow lost the fact that I am all His too!

My husband pointed this out to me a number of times, but it did not penetrate my heart. Thank God for my faithful, supportive, and patient husband! Eventually, Holy Spirit firmly and lovingly got me on track. He helped me steward my measure of faith in the truth of His complete provision, and it produced results.

It started with a simple instruction, "Pay yourself $500 per month." That took radical faith for me at the time!

After several months of that, the instruction changed to "Pay yourself $500 per week." Yikes! As much as I loved the idea of this, it was truly a step of faith to do it because when I looked at our cash flow, our operational and staffing expenses, and the projects that God placed on my heart that I wanted to invest in, the math did not line up.

I didn't do it right away. I did it for one week and then reduced the amount the next two weeks. I was finally paying myself weekly but doing the $500 per week was such a stretch of faith for me!

Each time I wrote that check out to myself for less than $500, I knew it was not God's best.

A month later I received a message from an intercessory prayer partner and friend: "Shae, as I prayed for you, I heard the word "commit"—it was the very first thing I heard, and I wasn't praying about any particular area of your life when I heard it. Then I saw the face of the Lion of Judah, and I heard, 'I'm serious about this.'"

I just love the faithfulness of God! I immediately committed to the $500 per week and saw the provision of God repeatedly in unexpected ways. One week I was compelled to sow generously into a woman's life who was coming to my city to speak. I decided that I would pay myself less that week so that I could be a blessing to her. I sensed an invitation from God to trust Him and write myself a check for that same $500 that I had committed to that week. I believed that He would cover my desire to bless this woman by bringing additional finances when I sowed into her life.

Whenever God extends an invitation to you, the answer should be "Yes Lord!"

Within 24 hours of sowing into this woman's life, Kingdom Driven LLC had an unexpected increase in revenue from our Firestarter School course as well as a contribution from someone who was led to sow into the work we do.

I allowed Holy Spirit to continue to lead me with the increases in my personal compensation, and eventually, I got a new instruction which was, "Push the envelope." At that point, I initiated my own incremental increases month after month by faith, and each time I would steward the unseen, I would feel an increased grace in the process. As of this writing, I am still pushing the envelope until Holy Spirit gives me a new direction in this area!

God is not only interested in seeing the vision He placed on your heart for your business to thrive in service to others, He also desires for you (and your family) to thrive as well!

Decisions about personal compensation, staffing compensation, business investments...all of these decisions are ones that your Ultimate CEO welcomes your invitation to involve Him in. Heaven's unlimited supply is available for it all.

I am a witness!

Lesson #2: Count the costs but move according to His Word.

I was sitting at my desk one day staring at a spreadsheet trying to figure out how to make the numbers work for a project God placed on my heart to do. I was counting up the costs because that is both responsible and biblical.

God interrupted my analysis with the words "You're doing your math. I want you to do MY math!" I paused at that moment to see if He had anything else to say. I was hoping Holy Spirit would elaborate. He does not always do that, but I was grateful that He did. I heard in my spirit, "Counting the costs, that's good, and it's wise. Count the cost, but this thing that you're working on right here, this is not about your math. This is about MY math."

This has happened to me numerous times with projects, events, films, face to face team retreats, and staffing increases. Each time I chose to believe God's word to me to focus on His math instead of mine and took faith-filled action despite inadequate resources, Heaven's unlimited supply showed up.

Most often it has shown up through unsolicited, favorable pricing, through contributions from people who want to sow into our work, and through people paying higher-than-average amounts for our Firestarter School e-course (it has no set price because it is offered at a "Pay as you are led" price... which, by the way, was a Holy Spirit-led decision).

Do the work of calculating the costs for doing what you feel God placed on your heart for your business. Know what it takes. Do the research. Get the quotes. Just know that you are not limited by your bank account balance.

Be led and exercise those faith muscles so that you are positioned and strong to go from one level to the next!

Lesson #3: You can make a king's decree when it is in alignment with God's word.

Multiple times per year we host Igniters Gatherings for those who are in our Igniters Mentoring Program, and during one of the Gatherings, Holy Spirit gave me three questions to ask each attendee. They scattered to find a private space to dream with God and seek Him regarding the answers to the questions. One of the questions was "What would ridiculous favor look like for you right now in your business?"

When we came back together, I asked the Igniters to share what He placed on their heart for their business that looks impossible and to share some crazy possibilities of what could happen (favor with God and man) to bring it to fruition. When each person shared their responses to all three questions, we would pray collectively concerning the things on their hearts, ask for God's will to be done, and thank Him for it in advance.

Sometimes Holy Spirit would give someone else in the room a specific word to share after we prayed. As one of the Igniters shared her response to the "ridiculous favor" question, I thought to myself, "she seems bolder and more confident than I'm used to hearing from her." She was not speaking loudly or forcefully, but there was a weightiness in her words.

Holy Spirit immediately said to me, "It is authority. That was a king's decree. Don't ask everyone to pray. When she is done, tell her that she spoke a king's decree according to my word and that all you are going to do is simply say aloud *yes and amen* in agreement. Then move on to the next person."

That was the first time Holy Spirit used the phrase "king's decree" with me, so naturally, I went into the Word of God to explore further and see what He would reveal to me. As I explored, I realized that part of stewarding the unseen is operating as a king under the rule and reign of the true King Jesus Christ.

A decree is an official order or decision made by a ruler

that typically has the force of law (unless there is divine intervention because God is sovereign and can turn the heart of a king as He desires). There are numerous examples of kings in the Bible making decrees in their kingdoms, such as Kings Darius, Nebuchadnezzar, and Cyrus.

As a Kingdom Driven Entrepreneur, you are a king in the earth realm with dominion and authority granted to you by God, and also subject to God (Revelations 1:6). When it comes to scriptural promises of God or the specific words God speaks to your spirit concerning your business, you have the authority to make a king's decree and to release that decree in the atmosphere over your life, business, or circumstances.

To be clear, I am not talking about making demands of our sovereign God based on whims or selfish desires. Your decrees as a king must be in alignment with the decrees of the King of kings. God says that His word that goes forth from His mouth does not return empty but will accomplish that which He has purposed and will succeed in the thing for which He sent it (Isaiah 55:11).

There is an entire heavenly host of angels that are heeding the voice of God's word, carrying out His commands (Psalm 103:21-22), ministering to you (Hebrews 1:14), and protecting you (Psalm 91:11-2).

Steward the unseen by making a king's decree for the work you are doing in the marketplace. Be led by the Spirit of God and His word concerning you. As you ponder on those decrees, give voice to them, and take faith-filled action accordingly in partnership with God. You will see that which God has said be accomplished.

A powerful truth that Jesus Christ revealed about life in the Kingdom with the Parable of the Sower is that a seed cultivated in good soil can produce 30, 60, or even 100 times what was planted. He taught that the seed is the Word of God, the soil represents our hearts, and good soil is a heart that hears and receives the Word, retains it, and perseveres in the faith.

As you allow the truth of the Word to penetrate your heart and you faithfully steward that Word and the unseen, you will reap an exponential, "God-sized" harvest up to one hundredfold!

REFLECTION QUESTIONS

1. How are you stewarding a vision of something in your business that you have very little details on and inadequate finances for?

2. How are you stewarding your time to do the uncomfortable things God has instructed you to do that do not make any sense based upon what you see?

3. How are you stewarding the measure of faith that you have?

4. What does stewardship of the unseen look like for you?

6

DREAMING WITH GOD: PERMISSION GRANTED

"Commit your work to the Lord, and your plans will be established."

—Proverbs 16:3

"It's time for you to dream." These were the words Holy Spirit spoke to me three years after starting the Kingdom Driven Entrepreneur movement. Those words came after two months of wondering why I was not receiving instructions from God as often as I had grown accustomed to when we first launched. It seemed to me like we had a good arrangement going.

"God, you tell me what to do with this business, and I'll be faithful and obedient to do it." I had never done business this way previously, and I was really enjoying growing in discerning His voice and seeking His heart for the work I was doing. I sensed a shift coming, and I wanted to go where God was leading, but I did not understand the shift until I heard Him speak to my heart, "You have my heart. Go and dream. Let's do this."

In that moment, He granted me permission to dream and called me into a beautiful dance with Him in business—a true partnership where He gave me wide open spaces to dream with Him, while He still maintained the ultimate lead position.

A couple months later, I received a phone call with a prophetic word of encouragement and confirmation from a friend. She said, "You're focused on making a prayerful decision on the next steps with your business, but God is saying that there is no wrong decision. It will be impossible to miss Him. If you choose option A, option B will come along with it later. If you choose option B, option A will still come along with it."

That was a confirmation of what Holy Spirit was speaking to me. I had permission to dream and to do, and my God, Immanuel ("God with us") was right there with me.

From that day forward, I embraced the dance of dreaming with God.

You have permission to dream. I'm going to repeat myself because I want it to settle in your heart. *You have permission to dream with God.* This may all sound counterintuitive to the entire first section of this book, which focused on hearing God's voice, following the leading of Holy Spirit, and being radically faithful and obedient.

I assure you that it is not. When you have a heart posture that is yielded to the Father, a willingness to hear and respond to Holy Spirit, and a lifestyle of communing with God, your pliability in His hands aligns your desires with His desires. You no longer create your own plans and ask Him to bless them.

God is actively present and ready to work with you on the things that He has placed on your heart for your business. His Spirit will continue to guide you, provide divine inspiration and strategy, course correct you, and so much more, but you will enjoy the freedom of imagining, thinking, creating, experimenting, implementing, and expressing what God has placed on the inside of you.

Too many Kingdom Driven Entrepreneurs are stagnated because they do not realize that God has granted them permission to dream. They are fearful of being wrong, making a mistake, and taking a risk when God has already said, "Go and dream and I'm right here with you." Do not be afraid. God wants to do business with you. He wants to release the Kingdom in you and then through you and the work you do. He has designed you to be a unique expression of Him on the earth. He has already equipped you by His divine power with everything that you need for your Kingdom driven business journey.

2 Peter 1:3-4, NKJV states:

"...His divine power has given to us all things that pertain to life and godliness, through the knowledge of Him who called us by glory and virtue, by which have been given to us exceedingly great and precious promises, that through these you may be partakers of the divine nature, having escaped the corruption that is in the world through lust."

Dreaming with God is a partnership with the divine nature! "Come away with me" is the invitation Jesus Christ gave to His disciples to escape from the busyness of the crowds and enjoy rest with Him in a secluded place (Mark 6:31-33). He is still making that invitation to you today.

Often the dreaming process only happens for entrepreneurs during annual or quarterly goal setting sessions; however, setting aside intentional time to accept the King's invitation to "Come away with me" and dream on a more frequent basis (i.e., weekly or even daily) will help you become a better steward of the unseen realm and work from Heaven's economy.

I urge you to sit quietly in His presence and dream about the needs and desires you have for your business to serve others well and reveal God's glory in the marketplace. Ask God for His thoughts and share your thoughts with Him.

Dream about the team needed to support the vision He's given you for your business. Dream about ways to have a greater impact in your local community. Dream about the types of people or organizations that would be ideal candidates for a Kingdom collaboration. Dream about the types of products and services your business can develop to bring greater value to your customers.

I think you get the idea. Dream, dream, dream without limits and self-doubt! As you engage your imagination, Holy Spirit reveals and aligns your thoughts with God's plans.

Understand that even as a Kingdom Driven Entrepreneur led by Holy Spirit in your business endeavors, your journey will not be a straight line. It will have twists and turns as you are planning, testing, and figuring things out all while God directs your steps. Be willing to explore what is on your heart with God without needing to have all the answers. He truly does work all things together for your good and His glory.

I'd like to close with a prayer of declaration of the Word of God for you and your business. I believe that His living and active Word will ignite your spirit and penetrate your soul.

I pray that the Father of Glory, the God of our Lord Jesus Christ, will give you the Spirit of wisdom and revelation in the knowledge of Him as you grow in intimacy (Ephesians 1:17).

I pray that your work is produced by faith, your labor is prompted by love, and your endurance is inspired by hope in our Lord Jesus Christ (1 Thessalonians 1:3).

I pray that you will know and experience the immeasurable power made available to you through faith; the same power God exerted to raise Christ from the dead and seated Him at His right hand in the Heavenly realms (Ephesians 1:19-20).

I pray that your love may abound more and more, with real knowledge and practical insight (Philippians 1:19) as you operate your business by His grace and led by His Spirit.

I pray that you are giving God a return on His investment in you; that you are yielding much fruit with your time, natural gifts, spiritual gifts, and finances and bringing the Kingdom of God with you wherever you are (John 15:8).

And finally, I pray that your mind is set on things above, and not earthly things (Colossians 3:2); that your heart has such a revelation of the priceless treasure that is the Kingdom of

God that you lose any appetite for the world's ways of doing business. Doing business God's way is your only way.

Thank you, Father, for the extraordinary privilege of dreaming with you, creating with you, working by your grace, and revealing your glory in the marketplace through the gifts you have so generously given us by your Spirit. Thank you for blessing us to be a blessing to others. Thank You, Lord, for the wonderful inheritance and freedom we have in Jesus Christ. And thank you Holy Spirit for working with us and through us so that we and others can experience the Kingdom of God on earth. It's in the mighty name of Jesus Christ, the name that is above EVERY name, that I pray.

Amen!

7

AN INVITATION

I pray that this book has been a blessing to you and will be a resource you can refer to repeatedly along your own journey as a Kingdom Driven Entrepreneur. You have now read quite a bit of my own story with the first six years of Kingdom Driven LLC, so it seems only fitting to end by extending an invitation to you to join the Kingdom Driven Entrepreneur movement.

Kingdom Driven Entrepreneur exists to help entrepreneurs to be led by God in business, so they can experience His best and have a greater Kingdom impact in the marketplace. Following are the five core principles that capture the heart of the movement and articulate what God is cultivating through this authentic community of business leaders around the globe.

A lifestyle of working by the power of God's grace

We accept God's invitation to work by the infinite power of His grace and favor, working diligently in partnership with Him (in His rest) rather than relying primarily on our own grind. (Matthew 11:28-30; 2 Corinthians 12:9)

A lifestyle of radical generosity

We model our lives and businesses according to the radical open-handedness and liberality that Christ demonstrated to release the power of the Kingdom. (Matthew 6:19-21; Acts 4:32-35)

A reflection of unity and collaboration

We lay aside selfish ambition and independence to put the King's agenda first, knowing that nothing is impossible when entrepreneurs within the Body of Christ come together with like mind and heart. (Ephesians 4)

A lifestyle of honor toward and for others

We eagerly esteem and affirm the God-given gifts and anointing on others' lives, creating a supernatural flow of Heaven's blessings. (Romans 12:10; Matthew 10:41)

A reflection of God's heart for humanity

We choose to carry God's heart to the world around us by the power of the Holy Spirit who resides on the inside of us. (John 3:16; Matthew 22:37-40)

If any of this resonates in your heart, I encourage you to join us! We have a number of resources to help you on your journey as a Kingdom Driven Entrepreneur, including The Kingdom Driven Entrepreneur Podcast, our Firestarter School online course, Igniters Mentoring Program, and in-person live events. You can access these resources and more on our website:

www.KingdomDrivenEntrepreneur.com

I love you, and I am rooting for you to experience God's best as you seek first the Kingdom!

Shae Bynes
Founder and Chief Fire Igniter
Kingdom Driven Entrepreneur

ABOUT THE AUTHOR

Shae Bynes is a passionate storyteller, teacher, and mentor whose life and business was completely transformed through the power of encountering the unrelenting love of God. Her heart is to see marketplace leaders and families that are courageous, connected, and fully aligned with Kingdom purpose.

Shae is the Founder and Chief Fire Igniter of *Kingdom Driven Entrepreneur,* a movement that inspires, teaches, and mentors entrepreneurs to be led by God in their businesses so they can experience His best and have a greater Kingdom impact in the marketplace.

Shae lives in the Fort Lauderdale, Florida area with her husband Phil and their three beautiful daughters.

BOOK PREVIEW

Grace Over Grind:
How Grace Will Take Your Business
Where Grinding Can't

INTRODUCTION

"*Too many believers in business idolize hard work. They exalt hard work over the presence of God in business.*"

These are the words that Holy Spirit shared with me one day as I was at the beach, enjoying the sight of my girls laughing together as we waited for our family photographer to arrive. Two simple statements from my favorite Teacher, packed with profound and convicting truth.

In the world of entrepreneurship, *hustle and grind* is a celebrated way of life. Some of the expressions you'll commonly hear or read on t-shirts, mugs, and social media memes are "I'm on my grind," "Rise and grind!", "Team No Sleep," "I'll sleep when I'm dead," "I hustle hard," "Good things come to those who grind"..

The list goes on.

You may even use some of these expressions yourself presently or perhaps you did in the past. There's no con-demnation or judgment here. I used to run a website with a tagline that included the phrase "get your hustle on."

Needless to say, I get it.

Well-meaning Christians have modified the idea of hustle and grind to make it more Jesus-friendly which has led to phrases such as:

Pray. Grind. Repeat.

Wake. Pray. Grind.

Eat. Pray. Hustle.

Hustle for Jesus.

God. Goals. Grind.

Grinding for God.

Push. Pray. Grind.

The phrases are different, and they sound more spiritual, but the prevailing mindset is the same.

When you look up the definition of grind in the dictionary, it is defined as *requiring much exertion* and *excessive hard work*. Synonyms for grind include the words struggle, attempt, and strain. When you look up the definition of hustle, it is defined as *making strenuous efforts to obtain especially money or business*. This should not be your testimony, and quite frankly, it doesn't have to be.

You may be thinking to yourself "Come on Shae, these are just words... it's just an expression!" But the cost of a hustle-and-grind mindset (even if you pray first or say you're doing it for Jesus) is simply too great for Kingdom-driven entrepreneurs. There is a supernatural realm that many Christian business owners are failing to tap into because they are busy grinding; running fast and furious to accomplish as much as possible, as quickly as possible.

This is not God's best, and if your heart is to see the realities of the Kingdom in your business, your industry, your city, or even the nations, it's imperative that you create and maintain a lifestyle of working by God's grace rather than by your grind.

Consider the words on the following pages to be an invitation from Abba, your heavenly Father, the Ultimate CEO, and best business partner you will ever have.

It's an invitation to live and work by the grace that He has so lovingly provided for you to experience His best in your business. Notice that I didn't say your best, but rather *His* best. I'm talking about the Ephesians 3:20 kind of best; which is immeasurably more than all you can ask or imagine according to His power that is at work within you.

My prayer is that this book will either serve as confirmation of what God has already placed on your heart, while helping you to grow on the path you're already on, or that it will provide you with new revelation; igniting faith and action for a different lifestyle of doing business.

Let's begin!

Grace Over Grind
is now available!

Get your copy today at:
www.graceovergrind.com

Made in the USA
Columbia, SC
29 May 2021